The School Bus Mystery

Therese Shea

NEIGHBORHOOD READERS

Rosen Classroom Books & Materials™
New York

It was the first day of school.
Dina and Paul got on the bus.

"Hello, Mr. Jones!" they said.
Mr. Jones said, "It is good to see you!"

"Hi, Paul! Hi, Dina!" said Joe.
"Hello, Joe!" they said.

"What is that?" said Dina.
"Did you hear that?"

Joe said, "What did you hear?"
"Listen!" said Dina.
Joe and Paul did not hear anything.

Joe saw something fly past him.
"Did you see that?" he said.

Paul said, "What did you see?"
"Look!" said Joe.
Paul and Dina did not see anything.

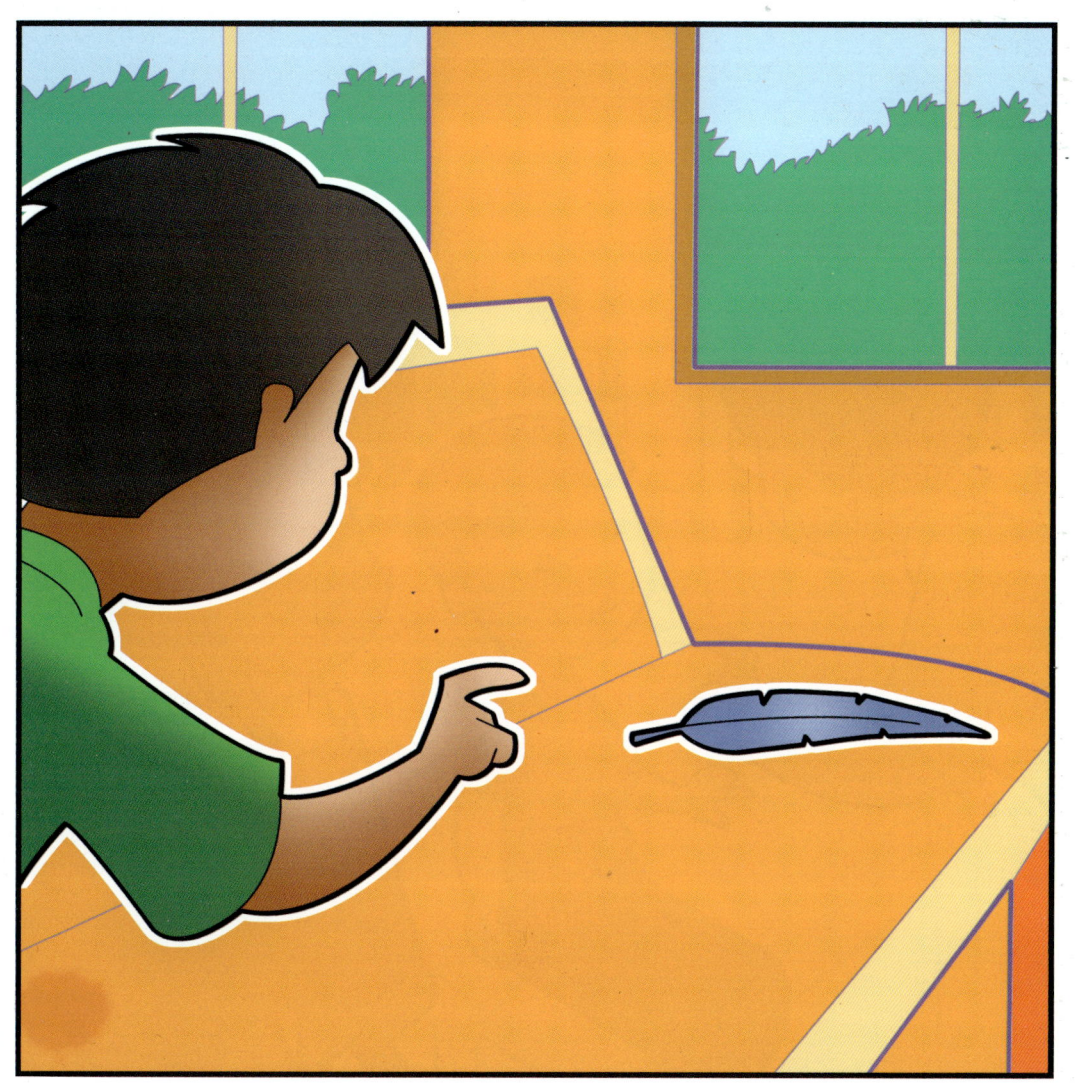

Paul looked on his seat.
"Look!" he said.
"I found a feather!"

"Hello, children," said Mrs. Wood.
"We have a mystery, Mrs. Wood!"
said the children.

"A mystery?" she said.
"There is something on this bus,"
said the children.

"I heard something," said Dina.
"I saw something fly by me," said Joe.
"I found a feather," said Paul.

"What do you think it is?"
said Mrs. Wood.
"It is a bird!" they said.

They looked on the bus.
They did not see the bird.

Then they heard something.
They looked up.
They saw the bird.

The bird flew out a window.
"The bird wanted to come to school!"
said Mrs. Wood.